WORKBOOK FOR

Practicing The Way

(A Guide to John Mark Comer's Book)

HERE, WE ARE MORE THAN DETERMINED TO SEE YOU ACHIEVE SUCCESS!

THESE ARE THE

CONTRIBUTIONS YOU'D MAKE

FOR EFFECTIVE USE OF THIS BOOK

- Realize now that deceit of self is a real and extremely terrible thing. Always remain sincere to yourself as you make use of this workbook, don't underrate or act with mischief when it comes to doing the task.

- Remain careful while conducting your search for a good and trusted person It will help you on this path.

- Remain very strict and consistent when it comes to doing the things you were told to do.

- Embrace the activities and constantly revisit when necessary.

- At the moment you reach the notes column, don't relent to empty your mind, thought and pain. Form new resolutions that bring change.

- Know that everything here is realistic.

YOUR FIRST DAY OF IMPROVEMENT EXERCISE

MANNA FOR THINKING

The greatest commandment above all else is love. In becoming like Christ and living your life to honor Him, you must understand what it truly means to love. John 3:16 "For God so loved the world that He gave His Only Begotten Son that whosoever believeth in Him shall not perish but have everlasting life".

THAT EFFORT YOU OUGHT TO MAKE TODAY

The act of love is the act of giving and sacrifice. If you truly love God, you must keep His commandments even when it's not easy to do so.

TIGHTEN THIS INTO YOUR MIND

How can you say you love God

that you do not see when you

can't love your neighbor that you

see every day?

OFFLOAD YOUR HEARTBREAK
AND OVERTHINKING

_____

_____

_____

_____

_____

_____

_____

_____

_____

_____

_____

BOLTEN THIS!

Love not the world neither the things of the world.

YOUR SECOND DAY OF IMPROVEMENT EXERCISE

MANNA FOR THINKING

In your work and service of God, you need to be committed to Him. It starts from a place of love though. Come into His presence with joy and gladness. Psalms 37:4 says "Delight thyself also in the Lord and He shall give thee the desires of thine heart.

THAT EFFORT YOU OUGHT TO

MAKE TODAY

It is never about what you can get from Him but about your faithfulness to Him.

TIGHTEN THIS INTO YOUR MIND

Remember that at this very point of your life, you have already done a lot for you. He didn't have to die but He did to give you salvation.

OFFLOAD YOUR HEARTBREAK
AND OVERTHINKING

_____

_____

_____

_____

_____

_____

_____

_____

_____

_____

_____

_____

_____

_____

_____

_____

_____

_____

_____

_____

_____

_____

_____

_____

_____

_____

_____

_____

_____

_____

_____

_____

_____

BOLTEN THIS!

Commitment and faithfulness draw the presence of God.

YOUR THIRD DAY OF IMPROVEMENT EXERCISE

MANNA FOR THINKING

Do this in remembrance of Him; when Christ was on Earth, He prayed to the point that His sweat was thick as blood. He was talking to His Father in Heaven. Hence, we can conclude that prayer is communication.

THAT EFFORT YOU OUGHT TO MAKE TODAY

Try organizing your time daily and ensure you pray always. Being intentional with God would also make Him intentional with you. It is a relationship after all.

TIGHTEN THIS INTO YOUR MIND

Prayer is a communication with God. Like any relationship you have, it needs communication to thrive. In the same vein, you need to draw closer to God through your regular communion with Him.

OFFLOAD YOUR HEARTBREAK AND OVERTHINKING

_____

_____

_____

_____

_____

_____

_____

_____

_____

_____

_____

_____

BOLTEN THIS!

Do not envision God as far from you. He wants to be close to you if you are ready.

YOUR FOURTH DAY OF IMPROVEMENT EXERCISE

MANNA FOR THINKING

Study to show yourself approve a workman that needs not be ashamed. One of the reasons a lot of us feel intimidated to talk about God with friends or even hide Him is because we don't study The Word of God

and you cannot defend who don't know. John
1:16

THAT EFFORT YOU OUGHT TO

MAKE TODAY

Your study time is just as important as work.
The Word is the breath of life that sustains
our connection to God. Study the Word of
God daily just as you eat daily.

TIGHTEN THIS INTO YOUR MIND

His Word is the bread of life that

you need to sustain yourself

always. The only reason you slack

off on it is that you don't realize

the importance.

OFFLOAD YOUR HEARTBREAK
AND OVERTHINKING

_____

_____

_____

_____

_____

_____

_____

_____

_____

_____

_____

_____

_____

_____

_____

_____

_____

_____

_____

_____

_____

_____

_____

_____

_____

_____

_____

_____

_____

BOLTEN THIS!

You cannot defend Him or live
like He did when you've not had

a personal encounter. You'd always tell the tale from another person's point of view.

YOUR FIFTH DAY OF IMPROVEMENT EXERCISE

MANNA FOR THINKING

Longsuffering is a fruit of the spirit. Children of God these days' claim that they love God and they want to be like Him but you catch the first flight when things get a tad bit uncomfortable.

THAT EFFORT YOU OUGHT TO MAKE TODAY

Patience and endurance are all part of the journey. It is a test of your faith.

<u>TIGHTEN THIS INTO YOU R MIND</u>

He is never late, He is always right

on time but in our impatience we

become our enemies and take the

temporal and fast road to our

versions of our dreams but the

results never last.

<u>OFFLOAD YOUR HEARTBREAK</u>
<u>AND OVERTHINKING</u>

_____

_____

_____

_____

_____

_____

_____

_____

_____

_____

_____

_____

_____

_____

_____

_____

_____

_____

_____

_____

_____

_____

_____

_____

_____

_____

_____

_____

_____

_____

BOLTEN THIS!

One thing Christ taught us was the importance of time. He was the savior even birth and He knew but He waited till the time set before He died for us. No rush, just the perfect time.

YOUR SIXTH DAY OF IMPROVEMENT EXERCISE

MANNA FOR THINKING

Be calculated in your speech and slow to anger. Even when He was buried by Judas, He didn't curse at Him.

THAT EFFORT YOU OUGHT TO MAKE TODAY

Emotions as validly as we need to make them, you do not need to live by them. In most cases, when you follow in the direction of your anger, you usually end up regretting it. Pray to God to help you control your anger.

TIGHTEN THIS INTO YOUR MIND

We can do nothing unless He strengthens us to do so. Ask for His help and He will help. "Ask and ye shall receive, Seek and ye shall find, Knock and the door would be opened.

OFFLOAD YOUR HEARTBREAK AND OVERTHINKING

_____

_____

_____

_____

_____

_____

_____

_____

_____

_____

_____

_____

BOLTEN THIS!

Anger, pride, when you live by
these things, you can never live
a life that glorifies God.

YOUR SEVENTH DAY OF

IMPROVEMENT EXERCISE

MANNA FOR THINKING

"If you love me, keep my commandments" ...
The only way to please God is in obedience
and abstinence from sin.

THAT EFFORT YOU OUGHT TO

MAKE TODAY

Obey His commandments and let them guide
your life daily. When you err against Him,
ask Him for mercy in sincerity and He will
answer your prayer.

TIGHTEN THIS INTO YOUR MIND

"Forgive us our trespasses even

as we forgive those who trespass

against us"... The Lord's prayer

makes us understand that even as

you want the Lord to forgive your shortcomings, you should be able to do that for others around you.

OFFLOAD YOUR HEARTBREAK AND OVERTHINKING

_____

_____

_____

_____

_____

_____

_____

_____

_____

_____

_____

_____

BOLTEN THIS!

To err is human, but to forgive is divine.

HURRAY!!!

It's joyful to know that you've

completed this program!

Don't depart from the things
you've learnt, Fix it deep into your
DNA.

Render love and support to friends
and family, send out copies.

Made in the USA
Coppell, TX
06 September 2024